C000176314

Fifty Year Stretch

Prisons and Imprisonment
1980-2030

Putting justice into words

Holloway Prison
An Inside Story

by Hilary Beauchamp

Hilary Beauchamp 'lifts the lid' on life inside, making the book a must for students of women's imprisonment. A unique and telling insight into life in a claustrophobic, tinder-box and sometimes violent atmosphere. An ideal primer on women's issues within the penal system.

Paperback ISBN 9781904380566 | Ebook ISBN 9781906534851

April 2010 | 256 pages

Youth Justice and The Youth Court
An Introduction

by Mike Watkins and Diane Johnson

Foreword Chris Stanley

A comprehensive guide to the youth justice process at a time of change. Covers both the youth court and the wider youth justice process—everything the reader needs to get to grips with the modern-day Youth Justice System (YJS).

Paperback ISBN 9781904380535 | Ebook ISBN 9781906534813

Oct 2009 | 272 pages

Full details and more titles at WatersidePress.co.uk

Fifty Year Stretch

Prisons and Imprisonment
1980-2030

Stephen Shaw

With a Foreword by

Martin Narey

 **WATERSIDE** PRESS

Fifty Year Stretch

Prisons and Imprisonment
1980-2030

Stephen Shaw

Published 2010 by
Waterside Press Ltd.
Sherfield Gables
Sherfield on Loddon
Hook, Hampshire
United Kingdon RG27 0JG

Telephone +44(0)1256 882250
Low cost UK landline calls
0845 2300 733
Email
enquiries@watersidepress.co.uk
Online catalogue
WatersidePress.co.uk

ISBN 9781904380573 (Hard-
back), 9781906534844 (ebook)

**Cataloguing-In-Publication
Data** A catalogue record for
this book can be obtained on
request from the British Library

Cover design
© 2010 Waterside Press.

UK distributor
Gardners Books, 1 Whittle
Drive, Eastbourne, East Sussex,
BN23 6QH. Tel: +44 (0)1323
521777; sales@gardners.com;
www.gardners.com

North American distributor
International Specialised Book
Services (ISBS), 920 NE 58th
Ave, Suite 300, Portland,
Oregon, 97213-3786, USA. Tel:
1 800 944 6190 Fax 1 503 280
8832; orders@isbs.com;
www.isbs.com

Printed by MPG Biddles Ltd,
Kings Lynn

Contents

About the author

Stephen Shaw has served first as Prisons Ombudsman and then as Prisons and Probation Ombudsman for England and Wales since 1999. Prior to becoming Ombudsman, he was director of the Prison Reform Trust (PRT) charity for 18 years. From May 2010 he will be the inaugural Chief Executive of the Office of the Health Professions Adjudicator (OHPA). As well as researching and writing about prisons for over 30 years, he has personally led investigations into deaths in custody, and chaired a variety of other inquiries including those into the Yarls Wood Riot of 2002 and the first public inquiry to be held into a near death in prison. He has also served as one of the independent members of the Parole Board's Review Committee that considers the cases of released prisoners who have committed serious further offences.

The author of the Foreword

Martin Narey is chief executive of Barnardo's—the UK's leading children's charity. Until 2005, he was Chief Executive of the National Offender Management Service (NOMS) and a Permanent Secretary at the Home Office. He began his career in the National Health Service before moving to HM Prison Service in 1982 where he soon became recognised for his commitment to transforming and motivating prison staff, clarity of vision and his determination to drive through improvements in prison conditions and the way that prisoners are treated, including via a Decency Agenda that led to significant improvements and reforms. In 2003 he was awarded an Honorary Doctorate by Sheffield Hallam University where, in 2006, he was made a Visiting Professor. He received the Chartered Management Institute Gold Medal for Leadership in 2004.

Foreword

I first met Stephen Shaw in about 1991 when, in an interlude
from the Prison Service, which was intended to teach me a
little about Whitehall, I was in the Home Office and setting
up the Area Criminal Justice Committees recommended
by the Woolf Report into the Strangeways Riot. Stephen
was running the Prison Reform Trust (PRT). I was struck
in that first meeting by how keen he was to improve things
and his willingness to accept that some of us working in
prisons might be as keen on penal reform as those working
in pressure groups.

Nearly a decade later, by which time I was Director General, and before Stephen left PRT, I saw that even more clearly.
When he visited a prison he would send me—privately—a
copy of his unfailingly perceptive notes. On one occasion he
'phoned me to tell me that I should visit Dartmoor urgently
and examine the arrangements in the segregation unit. What
I found was disturbing and I changed them immediately
before installing a new governor and setting in train a process of changing one of the most change resistant of prisons.
Stephen might have acted differently. He might have made
his disquiet over Dartmoor public or gone straight to Ministers. He would have obtained some impressive publicity
for PRT. But he was more interested in improving things
and was happy to sacrifice his day in the spotlight. That is
why, subsequently, he has made such a remarkably effective
Ombudsman and played such a key role in getting some sort
of a grip on the pandemic of prison suicides.

His short history provides an engaging and entertaining read. I joined the Prison Service in 1982, right at the beginning of the period covered by this book. I was one of the last borstal housemasters to which Stephen refers with some affection. But only just. Borstal was abolished just a few months after my tenure as a housemaster began. Why? Because overcrowding was undermining the concept that a Borstal Boy, serving an indeterminate sentence, had to earn his release. Little did I know how much that term *overcrowding* was to dominate my life and this history.

Stephen's conclusion is realistic but still depressing. I wish I could argue he is mistaken. I was not always so pessimistic. About ten years into the period covered here, and shortly after I became Director General of Prisons, I thought we were on the verge of fundamental change. Jack Straw was successful in getting me previously unimaginable funds and we were pouring that into prisoner education and drug treatment. In an intentional riposte to the poverty of the Tories' *Prison Works* mantra, Jack called his first speech on imprisonment *Making Prison Work*. We were making decency an imperative and sacking staff who so much as laid a hand on a prisoner. And the prison population stopped growing and even fell a little. We were able to reduce the number of offenders at one young offender institution while keeping the same number of staff in place in the expectation that we would be able significantly to increase rehabilitative activity and reduce re-offending.

But the window on success was soon obscured by the returning cloud of overcrowding. We were soon, once again, exerting massive effort at every level of the Prison Service in managing the population. The dramatic investment in prison regimes was caught by the numbers we had to incarcerate. Meanwhile, as Jack Straw moved on from being

Home Secretary, the heady optimism of the early Labour administration evaporated.

Eventually, I left the scene having failed to persuade Home Secretary Charles Clarke that without some control on the rate at which the prison population grew, the whole National Offender Management Service (NOMS) initiative was doomed. Legislation, meticulously brokered between Home Secretary David Blunkett and the then Lord Chief Justice, Lord Woolf, was weeks away from becoming law when David was forced to resign. His nanny and her fast-tracked visa application prevented what might have been the greatest reform of sentencing since the Criminal Justice Act 1991.

Twenty-thirty, the end of Stephen's history is still twenty years distant. Much can change and I am not without optimism that we might achieve a more rational and humane use of custody for children well before then. But, right now, three fifths through the fifty year period, things are not generally cheering. Indeed, politically, things look utterly bleak. We have moved from a position in the early nineteen eighties when Margaret Thatcher's Home Secretary was able to talk down the prison population, not least by coining the phrase: 'Prison is an expensive way of making bad people worse' to a position now where no politician, Conservative or Labour will speculate even about the possibility of reducing or containing the numbers of people we incarcerate.

For me, the lesson of this book is that until we see the return of the political courage displayed at the beginning of this history by Douglas Hurd when he was Home Secretary, we shall not see imprisonment, on any significant scale, providing for those we send away the genuinely rehabilitative, caring and crime reducing experience I still believe it can be.

Martin Narey
March 2010

Introduction

This short history began life as a lecture that I delivered to coincide with the official opening of the Centre for Prison Studies at the University of Salford in November 2008. However, I thought it might be of interest to a wider audience both to reflect upon the changes I have seen in the prison system over the past three decades and to offer some thoughts as to the likely direction of travel over the next 20 years or so. I have therefore expanded the original lecture into this current form.

I have tried to retain an informal, conversational tone. This is partly because I am not an academic criminologist or social historian and do not want to pretend that I am. (I have been a prison researcher, campaigner, and Ombudsman, but I have no academic qualifications in criminology or related disciplines whatsoever). It is also because whatever merit this contribution may have is in talking to a wider audience about some of things I have witnessed and thought about during a 30 year professional involvement with the Criminal Justice System. I hope that students and other readers who wish to dig deeper will be encouraged to do so. However, while I think that one of the underlying themes in the text is a significant one—that liberal democracy and a free market have distinct consequences for penal policy (and in some but by no means all respects, distinctly illiberal consequences)—I have largely eschewed the use of footnotes and references and other signifiers of intellectual respectability.

Small parts of what follows were first published in the *Independent Monitor* and *ConVerse* magazines.

Stephen Shaw

March 2010

Acknowledgements

My thanks are due to colleagues in the Prisons and Probation Ombudsman's office who read and commented on earlier versions of this text. All responsibility for the judgements I have reached and for any factual inaccuracies is of course my own.

Stephen Shaw
March 2010

Dedication

Between 1941 and 1945, my father was held first by the Italians and then by the Germans as a prisoner of war. He rarely spoke of his experiences but a single letter that he had written home via the Red Cross had survived and enjoyed iconic status amongst his possessions. He died when I was a young man, and I have always believed that his life was cut short because of the privations he suffered as a captive. I have also always hoped that my interest in prisons and prisoners is in some sense an act of homage. This book is dedicated to his memory.

CHAPTER 1

The Period in Question

CHAPTER 1

The Period in Question

Journalists readily parcel up time into decades: The Noughties, The Swinging Sixties, The Roaring Twenties, and so on. In everyday life, most of us also count back our lives ten years at a time. I talk about being born in the 1950s. Mrs. Thatcher was accused of taking the country back to the 1930s. A more prosperous decade is conjured up in the banal dinner party chitter-chatter, 'And what were you doing in the 1980s?' But of course history itself pays no regard to the date. To take just two examples: the early 1960s were very far from swinging (the misanthropic poet, Philip Larkin, famously wrote that sexual intercourse did not begin until 1963), and the second half of the 1930s was actually a period of significant economic growth. There is thus no magic in the five decade period that is the subject of this brief history of English penal policy.

I chose the first date as it more or less coincided with my own earliest involvement with the penal system. In 1979, I joined the National Association for the Care and Resettlement of Offenders (Nacro) and made my first visit to a prison shortly thereafter (although not before having opined on the iniquities of the prison system on national television: such is the self-confidence of youth). The prison I visited was Wormwood Scrubs—a good choice for a prison reformer as plaster busts of John Howard and Elizabeth Fry are embedded above the gate. It was not long after a major riot on D-Wing that housed those serving life sentences, and it was still necessary on the bottom landing to walk close to the wall for fear that a prisoner on one of those above would lob a battery or some other makeshift weapon at those below. (One did but he missed.)

I chose the second date more on a whim: a span of 50 years has no more historical significance than any other but it assuredly has a rhetorical ring to it. And 2030 is sufficiently far ahead to test my powers of prophesy without being so far distant as to render the exercise purposeless. Although it is likely that my own involvement with the penal system will then be long past, that is not true of many of those now working within prisons or thinking and writing about them.

There is also a rough-and-ready symmetry about the period 1980-2030; we are just over half-way through it with sufficient events in the past to analyse and sufficient time in the future to speculate upon. Indeed, if some of the rather pessimistic conclusions I have reached cause readers surprise or alarm, there is sufficient time to shape and change that future. I have always rather liked Karl Marx's dictum that the point of philosophy is not to interpret the world but to change it. (It is a youthful dictum; Marx was still in his twenties at the time he penned it.)

A period of 50 years also has a sort of conventional charm, and I admit to having found the title amusing. So 1980-2030 it is. But I must emphasise that there is no particular significance about the dates beyond what I have explained here, and in fact I begin my story rather earlier.

I have hinted already that some conclusions will not make the happiest reading for those who believe that our use of imprisonment is already excessive—whether in terms of its putative impact on crime or because it represents a quantum of pain that is itself a form of social harm. In coming to those conclusions and as a structure for what follows, I have drawn from ('stolen from' might be the more apt phrase) Francis Fukuyama's famous treatise *The End of History and the Last Man* (1992). Fukuyama's theme was that western liberal democracy represented the end state for human ideology and the form of government best suited to deliver the things that people want. The 'end of history' did not mean of course that it was the end of events. It did not mean that nothing more was going to happen. The idea (which turned Marxian theory on its head) was that liberal democracy and a free market had *proved* themselves as being the most effective way of allocating resources and making choices, and thus of maximising human happiness.

Leaving aside whether liberal capitalist democracy really is the end state of history or not, the question that I have asked myself is what its current triumph has meant for crime and the penal response to crime. To run ahead of ourselves somewhat, what liberal democracies seem to want are large, reasonably decent, reasonably purposeful prisons, delivered by a mixed market of public and private suppliers, increasingly reliant on technology, and with long sentences imposed by the courts thus trapping the most marginalised members of society. That may be a slightly Anglo-centric view (it does not entirely fit with the position in Scandinavia or in some other parts of Europe). But it does seem to me that it more or less describes the situation that we have reached in England in what my friend, the distinguished prison researcher Professor Alison Liebling, has called 'the late modern' prison system. In other words, democracy has reduced whatever tolerance there may once have been for crime and, as a result, has been bad news for those in the social groups most at risk of imprisonment. But the prisons themselves have been cleaned up and have become more just. They have become in many instances repositories of care for the addicted, the vulnerable, the elderly and the mentally ill. The Prison Service is not just a criminal justice agency. It has become a de facto social service.

So perhaps I may re-phrase Mr Fukuyama in the following manner: Is the late modern prison system the end of history so far as penal policy is concerned? Or to pose the question in a different and more down-to-earth way: What is it that 21st century penal reformers now want of the prison system, other than that there should be rather less recourse to it? Beyond tinkering at the edges, what reforms to the prison as an institution remain to be achieved? Moreover, is the reformist goal today of significantly reducing the number of people in prison any less distant than was the radical vision of abolitionism at the height of its vogue in the 1970s and 1980s? For while the size of the prison population may ebb and flow from year-to-year, is there any realistic prospect of the largescale decarceration that would reduce the number of prisoners from the present level of over 84,000 to the average of 40,000 or so that existed in 1980?

In most accounts of the purpose of imprisonment, gaols are supposed to deliver a range of utilitarian benefits: incapacitation, deterrence, rehabilitation, as well as symbolic ones like punishment and excoriation. In the middle years of this history, something about the purpose of prison—and of the entire Criminal Justice System—began to coalesce around the single term 'public protection'. (It would be interesting to know when exactly those words first entered the penal lexicon.) In itself public protection is of course a very good thing. If the State cannot protect its citizens there is a danger they will take the law into their own hands. Indeed, if the State cannot protect them, then people may wonder what the State is for at all. But if prisons exist to protect the public, how and why have they retained a moral core to their work in the treatment of prisoners? Why have they not regressed into mere human warehouses?

I shall try to address these questions by telling a story of English prisons over the 50-year period I have chosen. But if I am right in my basic thesis, I could have taken 2005, 2010, 2020, or virtually any other year after 2000 as the end date.

My theme presents an obvious challenge in trying to fit 50 years into a short but meaningful work. I should acknowledge at the outset that I will have relatively little to say on such important matters as the treatment of juveniles and young offenders, and very little on women's imprisonment, on race and diversity issues, and on healthcare. And although I first joined Nacro as an economist, I shall also have little to say about the costs of prisons over the period, and will make only limited references to privatisation, agency status (the idea, more honoured in the breach than the observance, that the Prison Service should be operationally independent of politicians), and the development of the National Offender Management Service (NOMS) in both its initial and current guise.

CHAPTER 2

Before the Flood

CHAPTER 2

Before the Flood

I should like to begin by offering a brief perspective on the period before the start date of this history. In other words, what was the state of the prisons in the first three-quarters of the 20th century? What is the pre-history so to speak?

The first thing to say is that for most of the 20th century, the Prison Service in England was a Cinderella service. It was not very interesting to the politicians or to the public or indeed to academics. The study of criminology in this country was more or less invented after the Second World War, and did not really exist as an English academic discipline beforehand. Indeed, the great names: Mannheim, Grunhut, and Radzinowicz, betray the continental origins of criminology as a subject of social science. Penology, which can be thought of as criminology's little cousin, also hardly existed. Save for the still-readable *English Prisons Today* (1922) by Stephen Hobhouse and Fenner Brockway, two socialists who had been imprisoned as conscientious objectors during the Great War, you are hard-pressed to find many books on prisons before the Second World War but for some execrable memoirs. Indeed, a famous riot at Dartmoor aside, it was a period when there was very little happening. It was a time when the prison population was stable or was actually falling. Many of the prisons now in use were actually closed in the inter-war period.

Likewise, if you look at what politicians had to say about prisons in the first three-quarters of the 20th century, there is very little to be found beyond Winston Churchill's reforming zeal during his brief period—February 1910–October 1911—as Home Secretary. A famous speech on 20 July 1910 in the House of Commons in which he said that the mood and tenor of a nation can be judged by the way it treats its criminals is still much quoted and also resonates today. (I am told that there is a similar line in Dostoyevsky, so either Churchill appropriated it for his own use or here is proof that great men think alike.)

As to English prisons in this period of pre-history, they were run under traditions dating back to the 19th century British Army. (Sir Edmund Du Cane and Sir Joshua Jebb, the physical and metaphorical architects of Victorian prisons, were both officers in the Royal Engineers. Their names live on in the postal addresses of Wormwood Scrubs and Brixton Prisons respectively.) Prison officers' uniforms reflected the military background from which many had been recruited, and the officers looked to the Chief Officer (a figure much like a Regimental Sergeant Major and equally to be feared) as much as to the Governor. There was no cross-over from the uniformed to the Governor grades.

Gaols were like individual fiefdoms or, bearing in mind the military provenance, like individual regiments with their own cultures and traditions. And there were individual Governors of great presence and authority; big men (except in women's prisons, there were no women Governors or officers) with big leadership capabilities. But mostly things were done as they had always been done. Prisons were run by custom and practice. Splendid old words like victualling (meaning the provision of meals) survived for years. Indeed, you can still find echoes of military procedures in contemporary prison terms like 'refractory' to describe disobedience or in the use of the otherwise bizarre word 'awards' to denote disciplinary punishments. (Most of us would prefer not to be 'awarded' solitary confinement in the segregation unit.)

The prison system was also what later might have been thought of as a typical nationalised industry. The 'nationalisation' of the prisons under the Prison Act 1877 was intended to introduce some uniformity in what had hitherto been locally-run institutions with little consistency between them. But in time nationalisation brought its own problems: the Prison Service was heavily unionised; it was very inefficient and, as a consequence of those two factors, it had lots of industrial relations problems. It was an industry subject to relatively little public oversight or interest; one where there was no real competition; and it was an industry where necessarily the producers (the staff) were in control.

At the same time, there was also a tradition of more-or-less benign paternalism in the treatment of prisoners—especially young prisoners. This is captured most readily by two names from 'early modern' prison history: Evelyn Ruggles-Brise, who was chairman of the Prison Commission from 1895 to 1921 and responsible for the establishment of the borstals, and Alexander Paterson, who had brought to bear his kindly but disciplined, Christian sympathies to the care of delinquent boys before World War One, and became Director of Convict Prisons from 1922 to 1946.

The borstal system was the exemplar of benign paternalism. I well remember old Prison Service hands who looked back to their time as borstal housemasters (a splendid word, redolent of the public schools) with real affection. There was certainly a more optimistic view of young people than exists today, and the regime involved large elements of fresh air and physical activity. In the 1930s, the borstal at Lowd-ham Grange in Nottinghamshire (now replaced by an adult prison) was actually built by boys from Feltham Borstal who had marched from London in an echo of the great unemployed marches of the time. This also happened at North Sea Camp.

There is of course a counter-history of the borstals which you can find in Brendan Behan's *Borstal Boy* and in Alan Sillitoe's *The Loneliness of the Long Distance Runner*. These novels suggest that things were not quite as kindly as the official accounts (and the memories of old men) might have had you believe. It may have been good for those who liked Outward Bound-style activities, but woebetide those who rebelled. Nevertheless, the re-badging of borstals—first as youth custody centres, then as young offender institutions—which occurred just after the starting point for this history did mark a loss of faith in rehabilitation, and a less sympa-thetic reading of the roots of offending by young people. Whatever faults they may have had, no borstal housemaster referred to his charges as 'feral', or gave them dehumanising nicknames like 'Rat-Boy'.

As the 20th century passed, so the decline in prison popu-lations between the wars was replaced by a gentle expansion. The numbers in prison doubled in the 15 years between 1945 and 1960, albeit from a low base. And the consequences of relying upon a predominantly Victorian infrastructure manifested themselves in conditions that the Victorians themselves would have regarded as degrading and corrupt-ing. Many prisoners in urban jails were held two or three to a cell. The physical environment was poor and regimes rudimentary. By the late 1970s, 'slopping out'—the daily emptying of plastic chamber pots of human waste into a sluice, there being no other in-cell sanitation—had become a key part of the 'regime' in many local prisons. (More solid wastes tended to be thrown out of the window to be collected by a special works party in the morning.) In a famous letter to *The Times* newspaper in 1981, the then Governor of Wormwood Scrubs described his prison as 'an affront to a civilised society'. He resigned shortly thereafter.

By this time, there was little or no notion of tackling re-offending. Both the political left and right subscribed to a doctrine that 'Nothing Works', and this was the prevailing ideology at the time I joined the Home Office Research Unit in 1980. Interestingly, the most common British citations to the academic work on which this view was based refer to an obscure American journal that it may reasonably be assumed hardly anyone had read in its original. The author of that work, Robert Martinson, was subsequently to reverse his judgement that nothing worked, but few took any notice. Martinson himself committed suicide by defenestration in the same year I joined the Home Office. (These events were not related.)

The Undeserving Poor

CHAPTER 3

The Undeserving Poor

While their offences may seem trivial by today's standards (Churchill had sought to reduce the prison population by, among other things, preventing the imprisonment of young men jailed for swearing or playing street-football), those who were trapped by the prison system as the 20th century opened were seen as part of the so-called 'undeserving poor'. In fact, just deserts played little part in their poverty. They were the orphans, the homeless, the unemployed people who had gone through the workhouse (the care system of the time), those who had been in psychiatric hospitals, those at the very edges of society. And it was little different by 1980. Then as now, and as in prison systems across the world, those incarcerated were drawn from the least advantaged sections of society. Then as now, they were the unemployed, those who had been in care, those who revolved between prisons and mental hospitals. Of course, no one is forced to commit crime, and even the most damaged and disadvantaged offenders are to some degree the authors of their own misfortune. To suggest otherwise is actually to deny the basic humanity of those who end up in prison. But I take it as equally self-evident that every prison system—in effect, if not in intention—penalises the poor, the disaffected, the marginalised, and the abused.

There is a term that you do not often hear these days but which still informs public policy: the term (or principle) is 'less eligibility'. This is the idea that the feckless, the workshy, and the delinquent must be treated in a way which is less attractive ('less eligible') than that enjoyed by the decent, law-abiding majority. In the 19th and early 20th centuries (before the coming of universal suffrage), this was deemed necessary for fear that the lower classes would otherwise abandon their virtue and elect for a criminal lifestyle. In our more democratic age, it is more often found in the proposition that public opinion would not accept that prisoners (or other representatives of the undeserving poor) should be treated better than ordinary members of the community.

There is evidence that this notion of less eligibility remains a current one in the recent (2008) decision not to increase prisoners' earnings. Or in the policy (also 2008) to restrict access to PlayStations and to ban 18+ games entirely. In the 1980s and 1990s, it was colour televisions to which access by prisoners had to be prevented at all costs. I am not sure if it is apocryphal, but I remember being told that in the United States (where you and I could not buy a black and white TV for love nor money), they have had to have them specially manufactured because prisoners cannot have use of something that the law-abiding might regard as a luxury.

Leaving to one side the tabloid fantasy of prison as a holiday camp—as someone who has had the mournful responsibility of opening nearly 500 investigations into prison suicides, I find the holiday camp metaphor particularly distasteful— the prison experience is characterised by what I think of as 'necessary cruelties'. In other words, the restrictions on life, liberty and property that are the ineluctable consequences of incarceration: the loss of choice over one's location and one's activities, the indignities of compulsory searches, the limits on the form and frequency of contact with family and friends. These cruelties result from separation, the loss of autonomy, and not least from being placed cheek by jowl with others not of one's choice. There is Jean-Paul Sartre's phrase, *L'enfer, c'est les autres* (Hell is other people) that I have often felt very well captures what prison is about.

But in addition to those necessary cruelties, and despite the official paternalism, the first three-quarters of the 20th century also brought with them unnecessary cruelties. The worst excesses of penal servitude (hard labour, poor diet, little or no communication either within the walls or with outside family) had been ended in the years following the landmark Gladstone Report of 1895. But prisons remained places of execution; and they punished with bread and water diets and by flogging on the triangle. It is too easily forgotten that we did not actually abolish corporal punishment in prisons until the mid 1960s, well after the Beatles' first LP. (As a judicial punishment, flogging in England had been ended in the 1948 Criminal Justice Act, although it infamously survived on the Isle of Man for a long time after that.) As a punishment in prisons, it was relatively rarely used in the 1950s and early 1960s, but it is instructive that it survived for as long as it did.

There were other unnecessary cruelties: those caused by staff excesses. The beating up of the Birmingham Six (the men wrongly accused and convicted of the Birmingham pub bombing of 1974) by staff at Winson Green was not some aberration occasioned in reaction to the IRA's bombing campaign in the West Midlands. It was all of a piece with what you could anticipate in many a segregation unit, especially in the afternoon. At lunchtime it was routine for officers to repair to the club or staff mess and drink three or four pints of beer before returning for their shift. And in the days before the development of control and restraint (c&r) techniques (that is, a more controlled, proportionate, and necessary use of violence), there was a lot of wrestling with prisoners on the floor, some of it doubtless fuelled by what the officers had consumed in a liquid lunch. In August 1980, again at Winson Green, one prisoner was kicked to death by staff in the prison's hospital wing.

There were also 'welcome committees' for disruptive prisoners transferred from one gaol to another. The frequent movements were dubbed by prisoners 'The Magic Roundabout', after the television programme of the same name. In France, the same process was known as penal tourism.

I should add that there were one or two unnecessary kindnesses at this time as well. When I first visited prisons, unconvicted prisoners were entitled to a daily half pint of beer or a bottle of wine as part of a meal brought into them by their relatives. If you went to the gate of a remand prison you would see great trays of fruit and other goodies that had been left for the prisoners, and there were amateurish attempts by the staff to see if someone had injected alcohol or drugs into the oranges etc. (Sometimes they had.)

But not everything was either cruel or kind. Most aspects of the custodial experience were simply the way they had always been. They were hidden from view from most of the public, save for those unfortunate enough to have a relative behind bars. These visitors of course were not valued and there were no Visitors Centres to keep people from the rain while they waited to be allowed in. The visits rooms themselves were utterly disgusting (as they remained until smoking was banned): dark and dingy, a reminder to prisoners' relations that they too were deemed part of the undeserving poor.

So what would a time-traveller make of the state of the prisons at the start of this history? For even a year as recent as 1980 feels a lifetime away from contemporary Britain. Prison staff in 1980 were exclusively white (and in male prisons, exclusively male), many following a family tradition. At that time, the prison population was overwhelmingly white too, and nominally Christian. The word diversity in its modern context had not been devised, and black and ethnic minority people were not over-represented in the prison population as was to become the case over the next two decades. These were also the days before hard drugs (I exaggerate slightly, but both heroin and cocaine use were tiny in comparison with current levels.) And it was before the era of cheap aeroplane travel and the globalisation of organized crime.

In a Cinderella prison system, many jails retained the look and feel they would have had fifty or even a hundred years earlier. Likewise the crimes for which 1980s prisoners were being punished overwhelmingly involved property (theft and burglary, in particular). There were significant numbers of fine defaulters, remand prisoners and those serving short sentences. This profile was to change hugely during the period of prison expansionism that was to follow.

CHAPTER 4

The Three Crises

CHAPTER 4

The Three Crises

Three interconnected crises make up the next stage of our story. First and foremost, as the certainties of hierarchy and tradition came under challenge from a post-war generation of baby-boomers, the prisoners themselves began to rebel.

In America, the prison riots of the 1960s and early 1970s (most famously at Attica in New York State in 1971 when 39 people died) were linked to a wider civil rights agenda. Indeed, the Attica Riot was triggered by the fatal shooting in a Californian prison of a black activist, George Jackson. (Jackson's book, *Soledad Brother*, captures the link between prison reform and the radical civil rights movement. Bob Dylan wrote a posthumous song about him.) The disturbances in England lacked this resonance (and any celebrity endorsement)—partly because so few prisoners were from minority groups (in Attica, over half the prisoners were African-Americans, and a significant number were Muslim).

The first serious mass disturbance in this country had been at Parkhurst in 1969. It was followed by other riots during the 1970s (notably at Gartree, Wormwood Scrubs and Hull) and was driven by long-term prisoners. However, by the 1980s sit-down protests and other incidents had begun to spread to lower security and local prisons. In 1986 rioting erupted in some 40 prisons. Fortunately, the degree of violence and injury was far short of American levels; nevertheless, a prison called Northeye, near Bexhill on Sea on the south coast, was actually burnt to the ground. These riots of 1986 are not often mentioned in the literature, and seem to have been rather airbrushed from people's memories. (I got into trouble at the time for suggesting that some staff had behaved less than professionally. I am obviously pleased that this has been forgotten.)

These manifestations of prisoner unrest were all to culminate in the largest and most prolonged prison confrontation in our history which broke out at Manchester's Strangeways prison over the Easter of 1990. Disturbances—some of them also of considerable seriousness—occurred at some 20 other prisons at the same time.

The Strangeways Riot was highly telegenic—and pictures of prisoners sitting out on the roof and systematically destroying it tile by tile were beamed all over the world. It was thus a national and political embarrassment as well as a symbol of the impotence of the prison authorities. The one television interview given by the Director General of the Prison Service, a decent but rather old-school civil servant called Chris Train, was widely ridiculed. It is impossible now to imagine a riot lasting 25 days with the head of the Prison Service giving just one TV interview. But such were the days when the prisons were run by a career bureaucrat and 24-hour news had not yet been invented.

The official response to the Strangeways Riot was a 600 page dissection of the prison system which became known as the Woolf Report (*Prison Disturbances April 1990: Report of an Inquiry*). Its authors, Lord Woolf and Sir Stephen Tumim (the then Chief Inspector of Prisons), exposed to public view just how antiquated the prison system had become. They castigated the overcrowding, poor conditions, weak management, and the lack of justice in the treatment of prisoners, and made no fewer than 204 specific recommendations for reform. One of those recommendations was to lead in 1994 to the establishment of the office of Prisons Ombudsman as the independent arbiter of prisoners' complaints, a post that I have filled since 1999.

Although now betraying its age, the Woolf Report still impresses as the most comprehensive analysis of the state of the prisons of the past 100 years. And credit too to the Conservative Government of the time for accepting all of the report's key recommendations, save that there should be a cap on overcrowding. The Government's commitment was somewhat undermined by its statement that there would be no extra resources and that it could take between 20 and 25 years to effect all the changes (time is nearly up), but looking back it is impressive how much has been changed for the better. (I consider these improvements in more detail later on.)

The second crisis to strike the Prison Service was one of security. A predominantly Victorian infrastructure was no longer up to the challenge of late 20th century would-be escapees.

To English commentators of a certain age, the escapes in the 1960s of the spy, George Blake, and of the Great Train Robber, Ronnie Biggs, have a filmic, black-and-white character. The escape of a man called John McVicar was in fact made into a film. (The part of McVicar was played by Roger Daltrey, the lead singer from The Who. There is an interesting story to be told about why pop stars are asked to take the part of gangsters. Another of the Great Train Robbers, Buster Edwards, was portrayed on screen by Phil Collins; and in another movie the Kray twins were played by the Kemp brothers who were, at the time, in a group called Spandau Ballet.) In contrast, the subsequent escapes from Parkhurst and Whitemoor in the mid-1990s have not made it into popular culture (perhaps because the prisoners concerned did not make good their exit).

The escapes in the 1960s led to the development of a system of security categorisation for prisoners that has continued to this day. It also led to the 'dispersal' of high security Category A prisoners into an estate specifically designed for that end, and in which physical security was greatly enhanced. In broad outline, this system also continues to this day, albeit some prisons have left the high security estate and the proportion of Category A prisoners 'dispersed' into a predominantly Category B population has increased. These so-called dispersal prisons, a term still in use although no longer officially, were in preference to a single fortress jail (to be called Vectis, the Roman name for the Isle of Wight) that had been proposed by Lord Mountbatten in his report into the escapes.

Notwithstanding that they ended in failure, the escape bids in the mid-1990s (a group of IRA prisoners escaped for an hour or so from Whitemoor in 1994, and three prisoners got out from Parkhurst for a couple of days in early 1995) were also to have a major impact upon the prison experience. Indeed, the then Director General, Derek Lewis, a former businessman brought in by the Government with a brief to bring business values into the management of gaols, was forced out of office by the Home Secretary of the time, Michael Howard. And the official reports into these incidents were a world away from the liberal sentiments of the Woolf Report. The first (the Woodcock Report) castigated 'a disaster waiting to happen ... so many things were wrong, so many procedures and policies totally ignored and with such regularity that the escape could have taken place on any day of the week with the same chance of success.' Indeed, it emerged that the Whitemoor escapees had successfully smuggled the explosive Semtex into the jail, although in the event they felt no need to use it. The second report (the Learmont Report) said that the circumstances leading to the escapes were not aberrations, 'but symptomatic of the practices … throughout the country.'

The confidence of Woodcock and Learmont's judgements may betray the fact that the former was a policeman and the latter was a general. Be that as it may, since that time there has been an astonishing turnaround in the Prison Service's security performance. The Secretary of State for Justice, Jack Straw, has referred to a time when, if somebody escaped from prison, the civil servants did not actually go and tell the Minister: they just saved them up until the end of the week. (Again this may be an apocryphal tale, but it represents an underlying reality.) One person a day still walks out of an open prison not willingly to return (although this is on a scale much reduced from what used to be the case), but the reduction in escapes from closed establishments has been utterly remarkable. The annual figure is now down to low single figures. In reflection of the Prison Service's current security record, I note that all immigration removal centres are now going to be built to prison standards.

The third of the crises to hit the prisons was in industrial relations. Although having less immediate impact upon the public at large, the industrial climate in the prisons rivalled in its toxicity that in the docks and the car industry.

The vast majority of prison officers are members of the Prison Officers' Association (POA) and there is a strong sense of loyalty to that union. (Other operational services like the police, the fire service, the ambulance service, exhibit similar loyalties. The reasons are not hard to discern.) The POA became increasingly militant during the 1960s and thereafter—and it has been plausibly argued that this in turn affected the tendency of prisoners to take part in disorder. Indeed, the 1986 riots to which I have referred led directly from industrial action by staff.

The starting date of this history, 1980, was the year of publication of a major inquiry (the May Report) into prison officers' pay and the way in which they were brigaded. The shift systems in place seemed almost designed to be inefficient, and there were staff (known colloquially as 'overtime bandits') who would ensure that they took the lion's share of such overtime as was available and who, as a consequence, would work for many hours on end. Subsequently, Chris Train's initiative known as Fresh Start in the second half of the 1980s set out (successfully) to end the abuse of the overtime system. However, it is not easy to run an unpredictably demand-led Service like the prisons without some form of overtime, and it has since returned in the form of TOIL (time off in lieu).

The loss of overtime reduced the POA's bargaining power, and since the early 1990s the management response to the union's demands has generally been more robust. Industrial action has been made unlawful, although this did not prevent a highly successful lightning strike in August 2007 that brought most prisons to their knees.

These three crises of disorder, security, and industrial discord were amongst the reasons that politicians became involved in the prisons to a greater degree than at any time since Winston

Churchill. However, the fundamental shift came because 'law and order' emerged from the shadows to become a key element of the political battle. The politicisation of prison issues was manifest when Margaret Thatcher's deputy, Willie Whitelaw, was publicly humiliated at the Conservative Party Conference of 1981 when he tried to advance a more liberal approach to penal issues (Mrs Thatcher herself had appeared to side with the Conference). Whitelaw's successor as Home Secretary, Leon Brittan, was widely believed to have adopted a more populist approach as a consequence. However, that is only one part of the picture. Interestingly enough, if you look at Lady Thatcher's autobiography, *The Downing Street Years*, there is only a tiny mention of prisons: just a short reference to the Strangeways Riot. For Margaret Thatcher, therefore, prisons (as opposed to 'law and order') were not really significant until the disturbances in the year she herself was removed from office.

Willie Whitelaw himself came back to his party conference in 1982 to trumpet the ludicrous 'short, sharp shock' for young offenders, and a paramilitary regime was subsequently introduced at four detention centres. Predictably, the regime had no effect on reconvictions, but (less predictably) the boys themselves rather liked it. It was consonant with their own macho values and made the time pass more quickly. Nevertheless, perhaps the real turning point was not until a further decade had passed and the appointment of Michael Howard as Home Secretary. In a key passage in his speech on 6 October 1993 to that year's Conservative Party Conference, Howard spoke as follows:

> Let us be clear. Prison works. It ensures that we are protected from
> murderers, muggers and rapists–and it makes many who are tempted
> to commit crime think twice ... This may mean that more people
> will go to prison. I do not flinch from that. We shall no longer judge
> the success of our system of justice by a fall in our prison population.

This endorsement of the incapacitative and deterrent effects
of imprisonment became known by the shorthand 'Prison
Works'. Howard also called for prisons that were decent
but austere, and sadly there were all too many in the Prison
Service who heard the second but not the first of these two
adjectives.

Although the term Prison Works has often been derided
by his political foes, it seems to me that Howard's remarks
now constitute an unspoken political consensus. (Or perhaps not so unspoken. In the Autumn of 2009, I heard
Justice Secretary, Jack Straw, cite the rise in the size of the
prison population as a cause of reduced crime in a speech to
the Prison Governors Association. Explaining the reduction
of one-third in recorded crime, a junior Minister, Maria
Eagle, told the *Guardian* newspaper in December 2009,
'Part of the reason for that is that we are catching and lock-
ing up for longer more serious and dangerous offenders.')
In effect, it had already been endorsed when New Labour
adopted in Opposition the highly successful mantra 'Tough
on crime, tough on the causes of crime'. In 1993, the average
prison population was just 44,566. When Labour came to
power in May 1997, it stood at 60,131. This continued to
increase, and stood at over 66,000 by mid-2001. It is around
84,000 as I pen these words.

My own feeling is that this political involvement in prisons (a process further accentuated by the establishing of

a Ministry of Justice in which prisons constitute a huge proportion of the political risk) is linked to other changes in the public response to crime: phrases like 'zero tolerance', the punitive approach to anti-social behaviour, the registers of violent and sexual offenders, the growth of CCTV, tagging (partial house arrest by any other name), and more intensive community punishments. This is sometimes referred to as the 'new punitiveness' but I am not sure that is quite right. What we have witnessed is not just the growth of punishment, but of a clearer divide in the public mind between 'offenders' and the rest of society. Notwithstanding the credit crunch, the market economy has made all of us materially richer beyond the dreams of our grandparents. Most people have a car or cars parked outside our homes—homes that are packed with portable and marketable electronic goods. We appear to lead less social lives as well—so the street (especially at night) has become a more alien and frightening place. In contrast to the expectations of social reformers 100 years ago, increasing wealth has engendered increased crime and an increased fear of crime. As a consequence, law and order is one of the few areas of life where the electorate welcome the State exercising greater powers and seem willing to pay for extra services. Private investment in crime control has also mushroomed. There are said to be more private security guards than police officers, every house has its burglar alarm, 'gated communities' are built to protect the wealthy and famous.

Of course, there is a lot of hypocrisy in all of this. One third of men have a criminal conviction to their name, and most of the remainder have only escaped one by good fortune rather than by good behaviour. Middle-class offending (tax and insurance fraud, for example) goes largely unchecked, and as people grow older so the memories of their own youthful indiscretions fade. The Teddy Boys and Mods and Rockers of the 1950s and 1960s are now doting grandparents, alarmed by new youth phenomena like Chavs and Hoodies. And, as it happens, the economic good times of the 1990s and the first five years of the new millennium coincided with a significant fall in volume crimes like burglary and car theft, while the social harm that resulted from the actions and inactions of large corporations and banks surely outweighed the depredations of teenage high jinks and delinquency.

Nevertheless, there can be little doubt that a seismic change of mood has taken place. And solely to interpret it as representing punitiveness strikes me as partial and misleading. The new democratic mood derives as much from a desire for protection (protection of our larger number of material goods, and protection of ourselves and our children), and this is a much more subtle, understandable and pardonable objective than a lust for punishment for its own sake. While the added protection provided by law and order services (whether public or private), by an escalating prison population, and by the development of new methods of surveillance and control in the community, is readily exaggerated, it is not negligible. Nor, self-evidently, is public protection an improper aim. Reducing the number of victims of crime is a laudable objective of public policy, and one which the public and the 24-hour mass media increasingly demand.

The extent to which politicians have responded to a different public and media mood—or helped to create that mood—has been much discussed (although in terms of the theme of this history it really does not matter which came first). A single turning point in England has frequently been identified in the abduction and murder of a Liverpool toddler, James Bulger, killed by two young boys when just one month short of his third birthday in February 1993. For what it may be worth, my own view is that it will never be possible to disentangle the relationship between public opinion, media representations of crime, and the rhetoric of democratic politicians. But while there will doubtless be mood swings in the future, I cannot now see a time when the politicisation of prisons and prison policy will cease to be a fact of life. If a period like the last ten years—when property crime has fallen significantly—has not loosened the political ties, I do not believe that it is likely to happen as and when crime starts to rise in the straitened times now facing the world economy.

With the triumph of liberal democracy has come a narrowing of the ideological divide between political parties. In those circumstances, no electorally ambitious politician would willingly be outflanked on law and order and public protection. The very idea of tolerance seems to have become a dirty word. The slogan 'zero tolerance' (whether applied to domestic violence, or homophobia, or drugs, or school indiscipline—to take just some of the first links found via Google)—implies that tolerance itself is a bad thing, for those on the political Left as on the Right. So just as there are now few real disputes between politicians on economics, or defence, or welfare reform, so penal policy too has become part of the great consensus. It is now time to consider in more detail what that consensus means for the prisons at the half-way stage of this history.

CHAPTER 5

Are We There Yet?

CHAPTER 5

Are We There Yet?

I have criticised the term 'new punitiveness' for its failure to engage with the public desire for protection, but I think the phrase is also flawed in that it fails to recognise how far prisons themselves have changed for the better. (To explain myself: that does not legitimise their increasing use, but it does call into question a thesis based on the quantum of pain alone). Let us start with what Woolf and Tumim said in their report on the 1990 prison riots: that it was the absence of justice (by which they meant both procedural justice and the more day-to-day sense of whether people felt treated fairly) that encouraged prisoners to believe it was legitimate to take the law into their own hands.

To a degree, some of the more manifest injustices were already being addressed even before the Strangeways Riot. The Woolf Report itself noted that restrictions on the right of prisoners to make complaints (a disciplinary offence of making any false and malicious allegation; another offence of repeatedly making groundless complaints; and a provision that a complaint could not be made outside the prison system unless it was made through the Prison Service's internal process at the same time) had all been abolished in April 1989. Strangeways Prison itself was in the hands of a bold, reforming Governor. But it was Woolf and Tumim who gave a major impetus to fairness and due process throughout the prison system. Personally, I have no doubt that the prison system today is much more just—both procedurally and in its commitment to deal with prisoners fairly—than was the

case before 1990. My own office of Prisons and Probation
Ombudsman, which was set up in 1994, is both an example of, and one of the guardians of, that additional justice.
The tripartite English system of prison accountability and
monitoring: Ombudsman, Chief Inspector, local Independent Monitoring Boards (each prison has an IMB made up
of local members of the public), is as comprehensive as any
the world over. Indeed, I emphasise the distinctively English nature of this system. It both has no exact equivalent
anywhere else in the world, and in a very English way it is
the result of historical accident rather than of any deliberate
plan. It is buttressed by other inspection regimes like that
of the European Committee for the Prevention of Torture,
further policed by a thriving charitable and pressure group
sector, and supported by a degree of openness in respect of
public information that again has no equivalent elsewhere.
The Prison Service's own website now puts into the public
domain all the rules, standards, orders and instructions by
which the prisons are governed. It is not so long ago that
these documents were treated as State secrets. Basic statisti-
cal information about the prisons is also freely available to
a degree that puts other nation's prison systems to shame.

In the wider world, the development of public law—
which to a significant degree has meant prison law—has
also meant that prisons have become more just places. The
removal from Governors of the power to impose added
days to a sentence for breach of the Prison Rules is a case
in point. Incorporation of the European Convention On
Human Rights into domestic law has brought additional
safeguards for prisoners, and important recent judgments
cover such matters as mother-and-baby units, voting rights

(to the great embarrassment of the Government, and not implemented in time for the 2010 General Election), and the investigation of 'near deaths' (suicide attempts that are caught in time).

Then there is what has become known as the 'decency agenda'. This embraces both how prisoners are treated by staff, the quality of regimes, and the state of the gaols themselves. The concept of decency was first promoted by Martin Narey (Director General of the Prison Service, 1998-2003) in his very first speech as Director General-elect, and repeatedly thereafter. A video was issued in 2001 which virtually all staff were required to watch. The aspiration to manage and care for prisoners with decency is a critical aspect of the late modern prison system.

In terms of physical conditions, prisons are hugely different from the way they were in the 1980s. When I first worked at the Prison Reform Trust (PRT) in 1981, the very paper on which prisoners would write to us was impregnated with a distinctive prison smell. You would open the envelope and be hit by a heady mix of stale cabbage, tobacco, urine and fear. It was part of the letter itself. You would encounter the same stench when you walked onto a prison wing. This smell is now lost to history like the pea-soupers and smogs of Victorian London. The atmosphere in prisons is literally healthier than 30 years ago. Prisons are much airier, they are much cleaner, they are much lighter.

The installation of predominantly integral (in-cell) sanitation is another result of the Woolf Report. I appreciate that ending the disgusting ritual of slopping-out may not sound a great step forward in a society where most people shower every day, and many houses are equipped with several lavatories. But it has contributed significantly to treating prisoners more decently. It has also ended the no less disgusting ritual of 'potting'—the tipping of the contents of the night pot over an officer or fellow prisoner. (Never underestimate the punitiveness—new or otherwise—of prisoners. Other ingenious weapons include batteries in the base of socks, razor blades moulded into the handles of toothbrushes, and a solution of boiled water and sugar that causes horrific burns as it adheres to its victim's skin.)

However, I am conscious that we still have many prisoners sharing cells with just a very basic screen around the toilet. That is hardly decent. The rest of us do not have to sleep with our heads just a couple of feet from a lavatory. Moreover, in a recent case that came to the Ombudsman, a prisoner who was in a single cell but with no screening around the toilet argued that this was not very decent either as staff could easily see him. I am bound to say I agreed with him.

Nevertheless, it is striking that there is now a generation of staff—including many uniformed staff—who have been brought up to believe that they should treat prisoners fairly. That they should address them by name, take their problems seriously, and offer kindness and support. I see this in my own work as Ombudsman when investigating deaths in custody. There are many more staff willing to go the extra mile: including with those prisoners who are difficult, demanding and dangerous. I sometimes refer to the Narey/Wheatley test (named after the current head of the Prison Service, Phil Wheatley, and his immediate predecessor): the question they ask of their staff is 'Would you accept this treatment or think it fair if it were meted out to your son, or your brother, or your dad?' It is a good test—both because of its simplicity and because it reminds staff of their common humanity with prisoners, no matter what horrors the prisoners may have perpetrated. It is a test that many staff would pass. It is a test that does not fit well with a philosophy of 'new punitiveness'.

Progress in terms of diversity has also been very striking. The staff group has changed massively in the last 25 years. There are far more women members of staff, more women governors, and many more black and minority ethnic (BME) members of staff as well. (Certainly in the London prisons, the staffing group increasingly reflects the population of the surrounding area. Progress in recruiting and retaining BME staff to work in more rural prisons has been slower.) There is now a support group for gay, lesbian and transgender staff, itself supported both by the Prison Service and by the Prison Officers' Association. And instead of going off to the mess and having three or four pints at lunchtime, you now find officers going off to the gym and demonstrating a very different approach to their work-life balance.

However, most BME and other minority prisoners would present a less encouraging view of the Prison Service's diversity agenda. In virtually every prison surveyed by HM Chief Inspector of Prisons, the responses from black and Muslim prisoners are less hopeful than those of their white counterparts. I am also conscious that a rhetoric of anti-racism can drown out all sorts of inequalities at wing and unit level. A bureaucracy of race equality can long co-exist with a hidden racist undercurrent. But while this is true, it is also the case that the overt racism of just two decades ago (prison officers sporting fascist badges, and slashing the peaks of their caps to create an oppressive image) is no more. Just as in society as a whole, it is facile to suggest that racism in prisons has been wholly overcome. But just as in society, it is dishonest to pretend that nothing has altered for the better. A lot has.

There has been more good news in respect of medical services in prison. I judge that the delivery of healthcare has been the biggest single improvement in the way that prisons operate today compared to 1980. There can be no doubt that abolishing the old Prison Medical Service and introducing the National Health Service as the commissioner (and usually the provider) of prison healthcare has brought huge benefits. There has been a big increase in resources, and prison healthcare centres are often now modern facilities that would not be out of place in mainstream medicine rather than the bleak rows of converted cells that they used to be. The quality of the staff employed has also improved immeasurably (to put the point bluntly: at one time, many prison doctors were people who could not get a job in the NHS). And specialist services like mental health in-reach have been developed. Contrast that with what passed for 'prison hospitals' thirty years ago. Dark, decrepit cells with sad wrecks of patients rendered comatose with large doses of anti-psychotic medication. Brixton's hospital wing, one of the largest and one of the worst, was known as Fraggle Rock (so named after another television programme for children).

I do not mean to suggest that everything today is fine. The new relationship between Governors and the Primary Care Trusts has not always worked well, there remains some reliance on agency staff, and there is an inevitable limit to the extent that prison healthcare can ever equate to the best care in the community. I am also sure there are still some areas that are under-resourced, particularly in the treatment of mental illness. Episodes of depression are almost regarded as ineluctable parts of the prison condition and thus go undiagnosed and untreated. Those prisoners with serious psychotic illnesses may still wait months for a transfer to a psychiatric hospital. Many of those with modest personality disorders will be lucky to receive any treatment at all. Nevertheless, the overall picture for prison healthcare is unrecognisable from what was the case. Years ago, I would visit a prison hospital and not infrequently find someone in acute distress in a pool of their own urine, utterly neglected. There is now no healthcare centre that would totally fail the Narey/Wheatley test. There used to be none that would pass it.

The whole resettlement agenda—the notion that some things actually do work to reduce future offending—is also a sign of greater healthiness in prisons, as well as being a feature of the end-state posited in this history. The Ministry of Justice has published research that analyses the factors linked to re-offending ('Factors Linked to Re-offending: A One-year Follow-up of Prisoners Who Took Part in the Resettlement Surveys 2001, 2003 and 2004', Ministry of Justice, 2008). It shows that getting people into accommodation and employment actually does reduce re-offending. Contact with a probation officer actually reduces re-offending; attending a prison job club actually reduces re-offending; attending a victim awareness course actually reduces re-offending. Likewise, the accredited psychotherapeutic offending behaviour courses that have been developed over recent years (notably, but not exclusively, the Sex Offender Treatment Programme) are achieving reductions on the predicted rate of re-offending that I would never have thought possible.

Among those released since 2000 from short-term imprisonment (less than three months), the actual reconviction rate has been slightly worse than the predicted rate (about 1.5 per cent worse). However, for those serving between three and six months, the actual reconviction rate is 1.3 per cent better than the prediction. For those serving between six and 12 months the improvement is 12 per cent on the prediction; for 12 months but less than two years, the improvement is just over 6 per cent. This rises in the two year to four year cohort to more than ten per cent, and for the four years and over group the improvement over the prediction rises to 13 per cent. (The scale of these improvements has also been heading upwards over the period.)

There is still a bit of me that wonders if the statistics can be quite right; have we calculated the predicted rate to take account of wider trends in society and in the economy? Has the police detection rate stayed constant, for example? Has 'target-hardening' reduced the incidence of opportunistic crime? Is it prison or post-release supervision that has become more effective? But on the face of it the figures really are very encouraging. They are about offenders' lives turned around, fewer victims, and a society potentially more at peace with itself. These are intensely moral outcomes, to be celebrated not decried. And there will be other areas of what prisons are now delivering in terms of regimes and programmes–to do with alcohol and drug abuse, to do with domestic violence, to do with anger and emotional control– where again there will be a good story to tell.

And the final piece of news suggesting that we have a better prison system is about something that did not happen. It is about how this country avoided constructing a super-maximum security prison, a place in permanent lock-down, a place of harsh conditions and sensory deprivation, like those in Australia and the United States. (Marion in Illinois is the best known; Florence in Colorado is now the only true super-max in the USA.) Instead, we have invested in specialist facilities: the close supervision centres (CSCS) for those deemed to be the most disruptive prisoners, and units for those diagnosed with Dangerous and Severe Personality Disorder (DSPD). I have borrowed a term used by a former Director of High Security Prisons, Mr Steve Wagstaffe, in referring to the close supervision centres and the four DSPD units (two in prisons, two in high security hospitals) as 'world class systems'. I am sure he is right. I think they *are* world class and they have helped both to ensure greater order and greater safety in the long-term estate, and to avoid the building of a super-max prison.

The CSCS are prisons within prisons, and like all specialist units they carry the greatest risk of going wrong. If the tendency towards abuse is ever-present in prisons (as I believe it is because of the imbalance of power—however legitimate the roots of that imbalance may be), then this is all the more true of special units for those judged the most dangerous and intractable. Indeed, when the CSCS were first introduced, I had severe doubts about their eligibility criteria and about the very restricted regime then on offer. However, the CSCS have been subject to a good deal of research input and this, and the operational experience that has been built up around them, now appears to have paid real dividends. They offer pretty reasonable care of those prisoners who genuinely are a danger to others, and a successful route back into the mainstream for those whose challenge is less severe.

Although there is always some mystique about specialist units, a key reason for the CSCs' success is that they have operated openly and visibly. It is an English success story that deserves to be heralded.

Likewise, the DSPD units are achieving something for a group of prisoners previously regarded as 'untreatable' by the psychiatric profession. It is true that personality disorder can be a catch-all, and its various typologies (which include exotic variants like narcissistic personality disorder, anti-social personality disorder, and passive-aggressive personality disorder) sometimes look tautologous. The long-term effectiveness of the DSPD units also remains unproven. But even if what the Americans would call 'correctional outcomes' are not apparent, the DSPD units are certainly providing a generally safe and purposeful environment for some of the most clinically disturbed and dangerous people in the country. In one of the units I came across a chap lounging on an easy chair, happily watching the television. I had last seen him being unlocked in a segregation unit by a team of seven Prison Service staff in full Control and Restraint (C&R) regalia. The DSPD units are another success story to add to the list.

To conclude, I judge that the reforms and innovations I have cited above do not fit well with a thesis based on increasing punitiveness alone. Rather they suggest a more sophisticated approach to the care (I use the word advisedly) of prisoners, one that is at times both kinder and gentler than what went before. There may well be public support for (or acquiescence in) a growing prison population. But outside of the tabloid fringe, there is no public taste for treating prisoners badly and considerable sympathy for a rehabilitative purpose to the prison experience.

CHAPTER 6

Secular Trends

CHAPTER 6

Secular Trends

I now turn to other trends that have manifested themselves in the current state of the prisons. I will look briefly at five trends:

- managerialism
- gigantism
- changes in the structure of the prison population
- its greater regulation; and
- the use of technology.

Managerialism

I will begin with managerialism—a development across the public sector as a whole these past 30 years.

In simple terms, managerialism is about the importation into public sector management of tools borrowed or adapted from private industry: key performance targets and other proxies for profit, project management, and so on. It is about getting away from the idea that prisons should be run on custom and practice, and that inspirational personal leadership is the only competence required of a Governor. It is about a new, more professional, more evidence-based, more audited approach to public service. However, many practitioners fear that it is also about getting away from the idea that prisons are different because of the human (and human rights) dimension. Managerialism thrives on statistics, but in prisons do they count the right things?

I am not a great managerialist myself as anyone who has worked with me during my career will tell you. But I was trained as an economist and do believe that some of managerialism's related initiatives have been welcome and have made the prisons more healthy. Of course, targets and tick boxes do not tell you everything. At the time of writing, I understand that Blantyre House Prison in Kent, one of the three self-described resettlement prisons, is in place number 113 on the Prison Service's 'weighted score card' (commonly, and not entirely unfairly, referred to as a 'league table'). On the face of it, that puts it in the bottom 20 per cent of all gaols. But this is a prison where they opened just one suicide prevention and monitoring (Assessment, Care in Custody and Teamwork (ACCT)) form last year; the year before they did not open any. It is a gaol that is famed for the strength of its staff-prisoner relationships, and one where the whole focus is on preparing long-term prisoners for a crime-free life on release.

The fact that Blantyre House is 113th on the weighted score card may tell you that there are limitations to the usefulness of the score card itself. But it does not mean that everything about a managerialist approach is silly or unhelpful. The idea of a comprehensive performance management framework may sound like business school gobbledygook when applied to intensely human institutions like prisons. But managerialism has brought real benefits: gaols are better audited and Governors are held accountable for their performance, there is more consistency, and more efficient use of resources.

I cannot imagine there can be any turning back from managerialism. And to be frank, nor should there be. Prisons consume large amounts of the taxpayers' money (between two and three billion pounds a year, depending on what you include). There is no case for inconsistent and wasteful use of all that public spending.

Managerialism is doubtless related to another feature of the public sector: the increasing involvement of private enterprise in delivering services for public benefit. Thirty years ago there was no private sector management of prisons—the very notion of prison privatisation had not yet arrived in the UK from across the Atlantic—yet today the prison system in England and Wales leads the way in the proportion of its prisoners in privately-run gaols.

There is quite a different essay to be written about why the private sector has made such headway in Anglophone countries in general and this country in particular. (So far as we are concerned, the perceived stranglehold over public prisons of the POA, and the Treasury's fascination with projects under the Public Finance Initiative (PFI) that take the investment costs off the public accounts, would be two important reasons.) Suffice it to say here that most prisoners report a preference for privately-run gaols because they say they are treated with greater respect, and that, by more objective standards, some of the private gaols have become first-rate institutions. There are also one or two poor private prisons—an indication that public or private management alone is not a predictor of what makes a good gaol. However, if the prison population continues its projected rise to 100,000 or so in the next few years, so the proportion of gaols in private hands will grow still further. Those of us who retain a visceral unease over prison privatisation as a concept have found ourselves on the wrong side of history.

Gigantism

Here is another 'ism': gigantism. (I have looked it up: it is a proper word.) And here is another trend of great interest to the prison historian: the growth in average prison size. In 1980, there were very few prisons with 1,000 prisoners. It would have been Liverpool, Wandsworth and maybe Strangeways, but I doubt if there were any more. Today, there are many prisons with 1,000 prisoners or so. And even our 'small' prisons are large by international standards. Ashfield—a private prison near Bristol which holds just short of 400 juvenile offenders—is at the time of writing the largest juvenile establishment in Europe.

All public institutions—schools, hospitals, prisons—seem to have got bigger in my lifetime. And the economic case for gigantism is self-evident. There are real economies of scale, and larger institutions can offer a wider range of facilities—including those of minority interest. But the objections also apply whatever the institution. Large schools are impersonal, large hospitals are unmanageable, large prisons have worse outcomes than small ones.

Prison size has grown mainly by paving over recreation areas and playing fields and putting in new houseblocks. It has been the equivalent to the practice of successive Governments of building on school playing fields—arguably the most counter-productive policy choice of the last 30 years, evidenced in the frightening levels of childhood obesity. The consequences in prisons have been less dramatic, but it is now a surprise to come across a prison with room for a football pitch on which prisoners' teams could compete in local leagues. It used to be commonplace.

Just as there are a lot more institutions with 1,000-plus places, so there is a separate phenomenon of the clustering of gaols to form mega-prisons. I am not sure if the Prison Service has yet offered a definition of 'clustering', but in broad terms it means the sharing of services between two or more prisons and the appointment of one overall chief executive or super-Governor. The best known example is the Isle of Sheppey cluster of Elmley, Swaleside and Standford Hill. In addition, HMP Hewell has been founded from Blakenhurst, Brockhill and Hewell Grange; the charming women's prison in the weald of Kent, East Sutton Park, is now linked to one of my favourite male prisons: the afore-mentioned Blantyre House; Latchmere House is linked to Wormwood Scrubs, and Askham Grange to New Hall. A cluster has also been established from the three prisons on the Isle of Wight (Parkhurst, Albany and Camp Hill), now brigaded together as HMP Isle of Wight.

To some extent, clustering is merely a logical extension from the way prison works departments (i.e. the people responsible for the upkeep of the fabric of the buildings) have been reorganized in modern times, with a single manager responsible for a number of gaols and a better matching of the number of staff to the work required. And it is I think self-evident that there are significant savings to the taxpayer as a consequence of sharing services. I understand the annual saving from the Sheppey cluster runs into several millions of pounds each year. Saving taxpayers' money is a good thing, but the more challenging question is whether clustering works institutionally. Do resources always shift to security tasks and the less risky parts of the cluster suffer as a consequence? And can Governors really manage split sites as well as they would wish? Perhaps one of the reasons that Blantyre House has apparently ended up as 113th on the weighted score card is that the Governor has to spend a lot of his time driving back and forth to East Sutton Park.

If there are question marks about clustering, there were many more about the proposal for so-called Titan prisons (gaols that could take up to 3,000 prisoners within a secure perimeter). The reaction to the Titans was almost wholly negative, and the proposal appears to have been mothballed. There were certainly many doubts about whether they would have been manageable, and subject to effective oversight, and whether resources within such a gaol would inevitably be drawn to the areas of greatest risk. The international experience of very large jails could kindly be described as mixed at best. Moreover, there is objective evidence that small prisons have better staff-prisoner relationships and lower levels of prisoner distress.

On the other hand, if the authorities are set upon penal expansion (the Government's current premise, and the direction of all the prison population projections), it may well prove easier to get a small number of large prisons up and running rather than a large number of small ones. Equally, it is possible that there may be significant economies of scale, although I remain uncertain as to how the practical difficulties of delivering joint services in a multi-purpose prison will be overcome.

My guess is that prisons large enough to take 3,000 prisoners are now off the agenda, but ones with anything from 1,500 to 2,000 places are still entirely feasible. However, it is to be hoped that we hear no more of the name Titan. According to Wikipedia, the use of titanic to mean large is based on a misreading of Greek mythology by confusing the Titans with the Gigantes. As for the Titans themselves, their behaviours included the killing of the child Dionysus, dismembering him, and boiling and roasting his limbs. Just the right image for a prison then.

Gigantism—whether by putting up new houseblocks on the remaining playing fields, or as clusters, or as 'large multi-purpose prisons' (the euphemism coined when Titans ran into trouble)—seems likely to continue. Indeed, a large multi-purpose prison can be presented as simply a 'cluster' with a perimeter wall. A cluster can be presented as a large gaol without the inconvenience of actually building one. Either way, there are potential financial benefits. But if size is inversely correlated with the moral performance of a prison, we will be saving money on one hand but achieving less successful outcomes on the other. I am particularly concerned about the impact on 'safer custody' and the consequences in terms of suicide and self-harm.

Changes in the structure of the prison population

I have already referred to the prison population expansion that has been a feature of the first half of this history: a doubling in the number of prisoners in the space of 25 years. But not only has the overall population grown; there has also been a significant change in its structure. The petty persistent offender (an archetype who was the subject of much research when I first started studying prisons) is now only rarely to be found in custody. The fine defaulters, the vagrants and the street prostitutes have largely followed the foul-mouthed youths and street-footballers of Churchill's day out of the prison system. (The phenomenon of secondary imprisonment—that is, the imprisonment of those who have breached a community penalty or not followed licence conditions following release—does continue to trap the more petty offenders for their persistence rather than the seriousness of their offending. This is particularly true of women prisoners.)

In general terms, the prison population today is increasingly made up of those who are serving long sentences for crimes involving violence, sex and drugs. Indeed, the length of sentences for the most serious crimes has grown to a degree that few would have predicted. In the mid-1980s, during his time as Home Secretary, Leon Brittan introduced a new policy that the minimum tariff (the shortest period to be served before eligibility for release on licence) for a life sentence prisoner convicted of killing a police officer would be 20 years. (The policy was to apply to some other murders as well.) This was presented as, and indeed seemed to be, an extraordinarily long time. From today's perspective, 20 years is mere bagatelle. If you use a gun to commit murder today, the tariff starts at 30 or 35 years.

Other offences—notably those involving sexual crime—are also subject to much longer nominal sentences. And there has been a proliferation in indeterminate sentencing geared to public protection (indeterminate sentences for public protection, or ISPP sentences, although sometimes known as IPPs). Because we have a mandatory penalty of life imprisonment for murder, England has more life sentence prisoners than any other country in Western Europe—in fact, more than the rest of Western Europe put together. When indeterminate sentences are added in, the mismatch with the European norm is even more striking. At the beginning of 2009, one prisoner in every seven was serving a sentence of life imprisonment or other indeterminate term. Although there has been some welcome amendment to the criteria for ISPPs, this percentage seems certain to rise further.

This huge change in sentencing for the most serious crimes has resulted in a significant shift in the way the prison population is constituted. The average age has also increased, and there is now a major sub-set of the population which is over 60 years of age. I recently came across a fellow in his nineties. Although it is sometimes presented that only those with 'whole life tariffs' (those 30 or so prisoners who have been told by a judge that they will never be released) will die in prison, the demography tells a different story. Increasing numbers of long-term prisoners will never be granted their release until or unless they have reached their end-of-life. As I know from my office's own work, some of them will then opt to remain in prison—preferring the world they know to the uncertainty of a hospital ward or hospice.

The stretching of the age structure in prison is just one example of how the population has become much more diverse. Every religion is now represented, with rapidly growing numbers of Muslim prisoners and, in the long-term prisons at least, an unfeasibly large number of Buddhists and Pagans. Every nationality is present too: from Afghans to Zimbabweans, with large numbers of Jamaicans and Nigerians, and a growing representation of Chinese, Vietnamese, Albanians and Russians.

Amongst British nationals, those from a BME or mixed race background are hugely over-represented. In America it is said to be easier for a young black man to end up in a penitentiary than in college. In many parts of our inner cities, the same thing is now true in this country. Indeed, if the rate of imprisonment overall in England and Wales is now around 140 per 100,000 total population (high by European standards but less than a quarter of the American rate), what would be the rate for black Britons? Simple arithmetic suggests that it would be well in excess of 1,000 per 100,000. Black Britons incur a higher imprisonment rate than that facing the citizens of the most punitive countries on earth. This is one of the most shaming statistics I know.

Mind you, it often surprises people to learn that some experience of imprisonment is not that rare amongst men. As I mentioned earlier, broadly speaking one-third of all men will receive a criminal conviction at some stage in their lives. This is in addition to whatever motoring offences they may commit. (However, there is a correlation between incurring motoring convictions and committing criminal offences, as the police are well aware. You can clear up quite a lot of crime if you go chasing after those guilty of minor traffic violations.) Again in round terms, about one-in-five of the men with a criminal record will also spend some time in prison. What this means is that between six and seven per cent of men will spend some time in custody at some point in their lives. This implies that in an average secondary school class of 30 boys, two of them will enter prison at some stage. Apply the same mathematics to a class in an inner-city boys school, and perhaps five or six will enter prison at least once in their life. This is also one of the most shaming statistics I know.

Women are much less likely to see within the prison walls. The chances of a woman entering custody at some point in her life are around one in 50. The female prison population more than doubled during the first part of the period covered by this history, but it has fallen back slightly during recent years and constitutes less than five per cent of the total.

The pattern of offending of women prisoners also differs from their male counterparts. A much higher proportion (over one-third) have been sentenced for theft and handling offences, and there is a lower involvement in serious violence and organized crime. Sexual offending amongst women is also rare.

The women who do end up in prison are likely to come from some of the most damaged backgrounds imaginable. Up to a half of women prisoners report having experienced violence at home. Many have suffered sexual as well as physical abuse. Nearly three-quarters enter custody with an existing drug problem requiring detoxification. A majority suffer from two or more mental disorders. Self-harm is at epidemic rates (the five per cent of the prison population that is female accounts for over half of all the self-harm incidents in custody).

It is a commonplace that women experience imprisonment differently from men: in particular, separation from children and family is borne more heavily. The overwhelmingly male character of prison is reflected in standard rules that rarely reflect women's special needs. Most reformers favour a new framework for women's prisons, with small community-based accommodation replacing the large gaols like Holloway Prison and operating under separate rules and management. However, this model has yet to win Government or professional Prison Service support, and it would take a radical change of direction for something like this to be in place by 2030. When Holloway Prison was comprehensively re-built in the 1960s it was genuinely believed that decarceration would mean it would no longer be required today, and would have been converted to use by the NHS. No such optimism seems warranted now.

Greater regulation

I have noted how the rhetoric around prisons has shifted to reflect an approach combining decency in treatment with public protection. I have suggested that this reflects a public mood that is unlikely to alter, and it affects probation just as much as it does prisons. Evidence for that may be found in how the police and probation now present themselves. Take these two strap-lines: 'Working Together for a Safer London' and 'Cutting Crime for a Safer London'. One of these is the strap-line of the London Probation Trust and the other is that used by the Metropolitan Police Service. Can you tell them apart? Indeed, I wonder how many people would guess that the first strap-line (the one with no mention of crime) is that of the Metropolitan Police while the second (the one promising to cut crime) is that of London Probation.

One of the recurring themes of the last 25 years has been a continual process of re-packaging probation and community penalties to try and make them more appealing to the public. Probation no longer sets out to 'advise, assist and befriend' (the words of the Probation of Offenders Act 1907) those who have broken the law. Indeed the word 'probation' no longer features within what is now the 'generic community sentence' of which the supervision that it formerly implied is merely one component. Under the Offender Management Model, an offender manager (the frankly horrid neologism for probation officer, and another example of re-packaging albeit one intended to assert the primacy of the probation officer in determining what happens to 'his' or 'her' offenders in custody) selects one of four broad options: PUNISH, HELP, CHANGE and CONTROL. The idea, we are told, is that the public will only wear 'alternatives to prison' (a phrase that itself begs a lot of questions) if they are presented as 'tough' and as suitably condign punishments.

The results of all this re-naming have been as dismal as anyone familiar with the science of brand recognition would have told those responsible. Does anybody know what the historic sentences of community service or a probation order are now called? Not one person in a hundred, I would guess. And why on earth are probation hostels now known as Approved Premises? As a result, and because people are not daft and know that supervision in the community—however intensive—can never be the same as prison, the re-packaging has very largely failed to win public sympathy.

It may well be that probation does have an image problem. But because of all the name changes surrounding the Probation Service, I suspect that most people no longer know what any of it is there to do. The Prison Service should watch out too. Which journalist in his or her right mind is going to talk about the National Offender Management Service (the NOMS Agency) rather than the Prison Service or Probation? Again, would one person in a hundred know what NOMS stands for? Would one prison officer in a hundred think they work for NOMS? In my experience, most still think they work for the Home Office not the Ministry of Justice. (So do many members of the public. I see from a photo of a demonstration outside Styal Prison in January 2009, held to protest against the suicides of women prisoners, that the placards read 'Shame on the Home Office'. Indeed, as I was revising this text in December 2009, I both received an IMB report addressed to the Home Secretary and read a prisons story in the satirical magazine *Private Eye* that had 'Home Office' as its headline.)

One other aspect of the changing face of probation practice is the extent of its involvement with the police—particularly through such initiatives as the Multi Agency Public Protection Arrangements, MAPPA. At a local level, probation and police now work together in a manner that would have been unimaginable two or three decades ago. However, at national level the services are further apart since probation moved with prisons to the Ministry of Justice while policing remains the responsibility of the Home Office. If its close cooperation with the police were better known by the public at large, probation's image might be boosted more quickly than it would by any amount of re-labelling of its products.

(It is perhaps not coincidental that the preferred discourse of the prison charities has also shifted over the years. Thirty years have passed since I worked as a researcher for the National Association for the Care and Resettlement of Offenders. These days, Nacro has re-branded itself as the Crime Prevention Charity and I am not sure it makes any mention of caring for offenders. The home page on the Nacro website makes has no reference to offenders at all; the page called 'About Nacro' has one mention of ex-offenders, but none about current ones.)

Just as probation practice has become more directive and controlling of those it supervises, so it is interesting to consider the extent to which prisoners' lives are now much more regulated than was the case back in 1980. Sentence planning on both sides of the prison wall via the Offender Assessment System known as OASYS is probably the strongest example. Prisoners are now expected to progress through their sentence taking part in courses and programmes designed to meet their 'criminogenic needs'. In other words, there is much more challenge to delinquent thinking and lifestyles than used to be the case.

Another example of greater regulation is mandatory drug testing, a procedure that has become something of an industry but one with limited effect on the prevalence of illicit drugs in prison. Most prisoners will take drugs if offered them, a reflection of their propensity to use drugs in the community and the desire to sleep through their sentence. Prisoners do not generally take party drugs. Their poisons of choice are those that have a soporific effect like heroin and cannabis. There is also a long prison history of brewing hooch—illicit alcohol—especially in the run-up to Christmas.

Other examples of this greater structure and regulation include the incentives and earned privileges (IEP) scheme, the aims of which are to encourage and reward good institutional behaviour. There are three main levels—basic, standard and enhanced—and where prisoners are on the IEP scheme is now much more important to most of them than the formal prison disciplinary system. This is reflected in the sort of complaints that come to the Ombudsman's office. In recent years, appeals against disciplinary adjudications have halved while IEP warnings and so-called back-staging—a reduction in privilege level—now feature much more strongly. IEP has given a lot more authority to frontline prison staff, but as in any discretionary procedure there is a lot of potential for misuse, inconsistency and improper discrimination. It is also questionable whether the scheme has achieved its goal of a more ordered prison environment, and in practice many of the IEP markings are pretty automatic. As often as not they reflect a prisoner's location rather than his or her behaviour.

Most prisoners would also cite the rise in the prestige of psychology as a further example of 'excessive' regulation of their lives. Certainly, the status of psychology within prisons has never been higher, but I do not know many prisoners who regard this development with any favour. The spread of accredited offending behaviour programmes like the Sex Offender Treatment Programme (SOTP) and Enhanced Thinking Skills (ETS) and others has provided many new opportunities for forensic psychologists, and has transformed the way in which a prison sentence is supposed to work. To achieve early release from a long sentence (or any release from an indeterminate sentence), prisoners must satisfy the Parole Board that they have properly followed a treatment regime and that the risk they pose has been reduced to manageable levels. The reports written by prison psychologists (whose numbers have mushroomed in recent years) play a very significant part in this process.

In the years after 2000, and following a series of public scandals involving prisoners released by the Parole Board, the Board's expectations of prisoners in terms of their engagement with programmes has taken off. The parole rate itself has fallen sharply. This reflects both a concern that prisoners had been released without a proper consideration of their risk factors (a concern to which I may have contributed, having spent two years as one of the two external members of the Parole Board's Review Committee that looks into cases where prisoners have been released on licence only to commit very serious further offences), and a belief in the effectiveness of the offending behaviour courses. The truth is slowly dawning on long-term prisoners that they are not going to be released early (or at all in the case of indeterminate and life sentence prisoners) unless they can show that they have 'addressed their offending behaviour' (another term, like public protection, that did not exist in 1980).

Technology

The final one of the five trends to which I wish to draw attention is that of the use of technology. As I have noted, all gaols are much more secure than they once were. The walls are higher, there is more razor wire, and more zoning, and all sorts of electronic wizardry is now in place. Technology has also been used to reduce staffing levels (through electronic unlocking), to reduce drug smuggling (through the Body Orifice Security Scanner, known as a BOSS chair), and to detect, monitor and prevent the use of mobile phones. Permitted telephony is via PINphones rather than cardphones, with much reduced levels of theft and bullying as a result, and providing greater control over misuse. Prisoners' visitors may be subject to palm print imaging and other wonders— especially in the privately-run prisons.

Meanwhile in the community, there have been major developments since 1980 in electronic tagging (the private sector contracts for which must cost many hundreds of millions of pounds). Although first promoted as a way of reducing the prison population, tagging has at best capped the rate of increase by providing comfort for those magistrates imposing curfew orders and a more structured release programme via home detention curfew (HDC). It seems fair to predict that more mobile (satellite) monitoring will come into place in the future—both to police things like exclusion orders and more generally to supplement static monitoring at home. CCTV coverage is also now widespread, and the current grainy images are likely to be replaced as high definition cameras become the norm. This will act as a protection both for prisoners (against wrongdoing) and for staff (against false allegations of wrongdoing). My colleagues in the Ombudsman's office already spend many hours comparing CCTV evidence with what staff and prisoners say has occurred. I am a particular advocate of CCTV in segregation units and other sensitive locations.

But amongst all this modernity, the old issues (the old trends, if you like) have not gone away. As I write these words, many prisons are critically overcrowded and prison regimes are under growing threat. Indeed, I judge that the threat to regimes is now greater than at any time since the 1990s.

One of my minor eccentricities is that I am an avid reader of Independent Monitoring Board annual reports. In the old days I used to scour IMB reports in the hope of finding anything but an account of the health of the prison cat, but these days most IMBs are properly focussed on the job they are there to do: to monitor the treatment of prisoners. Report after report from these Boards now refers to the threat to regime hours, and the inevitable consequence that prisoners spend longer in their cells.

There is a real danger that, as the financial squeeze on the Prison Service gets tighter—not just this year but in the years ahead—happiness will again be defined as 'door shaped' (a phrase used by prison staff in the past to indicate their preference for prisoners to be locked away rather than out of their cells in activities or on association). The financial squeeze also has implications for industrial relations—the problems of which have not gone away either.

Other parts of the decency agenda may also be under threat. It is disheartening to discover how late many prisoners are arriving back from court—often after long journeys in cubicular vans. Escort arrangements were one of the first services to be privatised, but I wonder if private escort contracts may be like the clustering of prisons mentioned earlier in this chapter: a saving to the public purse but a worse custodial outcome. Getting prisoners into gaol late into the evening is not a decent way of treating people (including children, for whom the delays are often worst), and of course it increases the risk of self-harm.

In her 2007-2008 Annual Report, the Chief Inspector of Prisons, Dame Anne Owers, wrote that the lessons learned during the 1980s and 1990s, and articulated in the Woolf Report, 'need to form the bedrock of strategy for the 2010s'. If the long-term prison population grows while resource constraints bite, 'there are real risks of destabilising safety and control, and of reducing opportunities for change and rehabilitation'. Although I do not believe there is any likelihood of regimes reverting to where they were in 1980, there are already some 'training' prisons where prisoner unemployment is high and little training is evident. Dame Anne knows of which she speaks.

Past Tense, Future Imperfect

CHAPTER 7

Past Tense, Future Imperfect

In this penultimate chapter of this short history, I will look in more detail at what the future may bring for the prisons. And the first thing to say of course is that the old issues are not going to go away between now and 2030. I see no likelihood that this country will succeed in building its way out of overcrowding. (I am not sure if there is any proper research on this issue, but I feel confident in saying that no country ever has.) In other words, the mis-match between the number of prisoners and the number of spaces (and the regional mis-matches which exacerbate the overall problem, some areas being net exporters and others net importers) is not going to go away. Given this fact, and the wider resource constraints, the consequences in terms of compulsory cell-sharing, in terms of pressure on services and regimes, in terms of safety and decency, are not going to go away either.

I do not suppose it is a saying much used by younger people, but you cannot fit a quart into a pint pot. In pure capacity terms, prisons are in fact remarkably elastic. You can, if you choose, have prisoners two, three or four to a cell, or sleeping in corridors or in gymnasiums. In Eastern Europe and elsewhere in the world it is not hard to find prisons where the prisoners have to sleep in shifts, there being insufficient beds to go round. (I have visited such prisons myself.) But it is much more difficult to cope with the turnover (the jargon word is 'churn') of prisoners from cell to cell, wing to wing, gaol to police cell to gaol. Nor can you provide sufficient activities to keep prisoners safely occupied and help them to lead more crime-free lives. Overcrowding is much more a matter of occupation than it is of the crude numbers. I share Dame Anne Owers' concerns about the impact both on prisoners and on society as a whole.

Given this continuing pressure of population, I believe there will be increasing attempts to achieve what in the City of London they call 'sweating the assets'; in other words, trying to extract the most out of the prisons that we do have. Gaols are expensive and labour-intensive. The emphasis will be on lower staffing levels, greater reliance on technology, more clustering and/or the closure of the small gaols I favour, and the paving over of any remaining playing fields or land that is not in use. The fall-out from the credit crunch and the world economic downturn will accelerate these tendencies.

Despite the abandonment of the plans for Titan prisons, the implication within those proposals of at least some decommissioning of inner-city gaols, and their replacement by larger prisons perhaps somewhere near the motorways, remains intact. The idea is that the gaols built by the Victorians are often on commercially attractive urban sites where developers would be interested in putting up bijou apartments. If you close the prison and sell the land, there should be enough to pay for a new prison with better transport links and perhaps a few quid left over too. (If you want a model of this, the football industry provides one. Many professional football clubs have sold their inner-city grounds for development, and moved to new stadia with better facilities and better road links on the edge of town.) There is already a prison example of a kind in that the ancient gaol in the centre of Oxford has been converted into a luxury hotel called Malmaison Oxford. Parts of the gaol dated back

1,000 years but it was still in use in the 1980s when I visited it several times. The prisoners who would have been located there are now in the modern prison of Bullingdon, built on a greenfield site outside Bicester, ten miles or so away.

Looking at prisons in terms of their asset values is a relatively new development. When I worked for Nacro all those years ago, my main work was a study of what prison sentences actually cost. To try and work this out, I looked both at the direct resource costs and the opportunity costs (in other words, the benefits given up because the money was spent on prisons rather than on something else). It was all very rough-and-ready, and I remember ringing round the local authority rating valuation offices to try and get a figure for what you would raise if you pulled down Pentonville or Wandsworth and allowed the developers to put up executive homes instead. I discovered that the Prison Service was sitting on some really valuable property. It turned out that an open prison like Ford, which occupies a large site near Arundel in Sussex, would be worth an absolute fortune were a housing development to be approved for it.

Entertainingly, the then chairman of Nacro, Tony Christopher, was the leader of the trade union for the very staff I had been phoning up in the valuation offices. I recall that he was absolutely furious that Nacro was employing a young idiot who was wasting his time ringing his members to find out what the value of a prison property might be if you demolished it. Nothing could have seemed more absurd to him. It is now public policy, while Nacro became part of a consortium with a private firm bidding for the contract to build a new greenfield prison. How times change.

As to the population to be held in these sweated assets, I have already alluded to longer effective sentences and the consequences for the number of people behind bars at any one time. For 60 years, the prison population has been on a broadly upward path. On what basis could we anticipate that over the next 20 years this growth in the number of people in prison is going to be reversed? Indeed the Titans and the current building programme were predicated on the population growing, and it would take a brave person to gainsay that prediction.

Of course, it is always possible that there will be a change in policy and sentiment of the kind that occurred during the first half of the 20th century. Perhaps the very cost of prison will prove a brake in a time of economic adversity—the Treasury never having been a fan of law and order spending, most of which it regards as wasted. However, for the reasons that I have advanced I think such a change is unlikely— notwithstanding the significant reduction in crimes like burglary that has occurred over the last 15 years. Except perhaps when they are used for women and juvenile offenders, the imposition of custodial sentences seems to make people feel better about themselves. Indeed, if the trend in crime reverses in response to the economic downturn (it may reasonably be expected that property crime will rise but alcohol-fuelled violent crime will fall during a recession), then this may actually reinforce the popularity of imprisonment as a response to criminal behaviour. A fractured, anxious, society is surely even less likely to embrace a more liberal penal policy than one that enjoys consistently improving living standards.

Within this growing prison population, there will be an increasing number of elderly or prematurely elderly prisoners seeing out their days at the end of long sentences. Interestingly, some recent research suggests that elderly prisoners may have a rather better life-expectancy in prison than they would outside—perhaps because prisons are generally warm and because there is limited access to life-shortening substances like tobacco and strong drink. Nevertheless, the 'greying' of the prison population has major implications for prison design—elderly prisoners have less need for workshops, classrooms and gyms, and may have difficulty using staircases—and for healthcare provision. This has already become manifest in some parts of the United States, and it is only a question of time before this country follows suit.

I have already referred to another feature of both American and English prisons: that of secondary imprisonment—the recall to prison of those who have 'failed' while on licence. In a local prison like Manchester (they do not like to call it Strangeways any more), I understand that no less than 14 per cent of the population has already been released once and then returned following breach of their licence. As licence conditions get ever stricter, and as enforcement gets more certain (perhaps through the medium of technology), so I expect that secondary imprisonment will continue to drive the overall increase in the number of prisoners. The more robust supervision of community penalties has had, and will have, a similar effect.

As we have also seen, globalisation is likewise changing the face of crime and the nature of the prison population. I see no reason to believe that the proportion of foreign nationals in English gaols is likely to fall from its current level of over ten per cent. Indeed, while the proportions differ from country to country, this is feature of imprisonment across Europe and across the globe. Crime has become international, and travel itself may weaken the hold of moral certainties. Most of us are more likely to behave badly the further we are from home. (Just consider the behaviour of university students, or of international businessmen, should you doubt this.)

Nor can I envisage a prison system that does not entrap the already disadvantaged, especially those from visible minorities. Again, this is a characteristic of prisons across the world. French prisons are full of Algerians and Moroccans, German prisons hold Turks and Serbs, the Roma make up the majority of prisoners in the Balkans. In some parts of Australia, indigenous Australians dominate the prison population. Likewise in Canada, native peoples are hugely over-represented. In the USA, well over half the prisoners in America are black or Latino. And so it goes on.

And as in the United States, in this country the various national, religious and ethnic groupings in prison are increasingly identifying with themselves. A related trend is that we are beginning to see the development of a gang culture in prisons that reflects a growing gang culture in the inner cities. (I appreciate that not all gangs are based on race, religion or nationality.) Incidents occurring on the streets are having an echo within the prison walls, and at least one gang murder seems to have been orchestrated from the inside. Gang identification cuts much deeper than the older tribal identification with city of origin (Mancs v. Scousers) or football teams.

I am aware that this is an acutely sensitive subject. The word 'gang' is not one with which most criminologists feel intuitively comfortable. It reeks of labelling and of tabloid simplification. I understand this, and I think it is important to distinguish between identification with a group of friends from your area (even a group of criminal friends) and the wider and enduring commitment to gang values or organized crime. However, it is also obvious to me that we do in fact now have, certainly in London and the larger cities, some crime gangs that are based on ethnic and national groupings. The history of crime in the United States suggests that this has always been the case there, but in Britain it is a more recent creation. (There are some earlier examples—the sex trade in Soho between the 1940s and 1960s was run by Maltese criminals, for instance.)

In some high security gaols, I sense there is a danger of de facto segregation in that there are wings that are predominantly white and wings that are predominantly BME. In part, this reflects differences in offence category (those prisoners segregated from others as sex offenders are predominantly white), but the pull of the gang—and the violence and intimidation associated with the gang—is undoubtedly a further factor. Religious identification and conversion (the growth in the number of Islamic prisoners being a critical trend of the past decade) adds to the complexity. It is unfortunate that aggregate prison population figures rarely capture what I fear may become a growing and dangerous trend. (You have to look at the figures wing by wing, or unit by unit, rather than at the gaol as a whole.) Ensuring that a racial and religious divide, and the bullying and radicalisation with which it may in part be associated, does not develop will be one of the Prison Service's major challenges over the remaining years of this history.

There is no reason why Britain needs to follow America into a racially divided prison system. Indeed, it is often said with some pride that this country has an impressive record of racial tolerance and integration. (A visit to the racially segregated former mill towns of Yorkshire and Lancashire may suggest a metropolitan bias in this happy version of reality.) Be that as it may, I think nothing is to be gained by pretending that the potential for racial and religious division does not exist within the prisons, or that it is a problem simply in terms of institutional order and control.

Who else amongst the disadvantaged will contribute to the rising prison population? People with mental health problems seem likely to make up more than their fair share. For ever since the modern prison came into being, gaols have acted as mental health facilities. I sometimes quote this passage from John Howard's *The State of the Prisons*, written nearly 250 years ago:

> In some few jails are confined idiots and lunatics … many of the bridewells are crowded and offensive, because the rooms which were designed for prisoners are occupied by lunatics … The insane, when they are not kept separate, disturb and terrify other prisoners. No care is taken of them, although it is probable that by medicines, and proper regiment, some of them might be restored to their senses, and usefulness in life.

If this was the case in the late 18th century, and has remained so ever since, there are few grounds for optimism that the situation will be overcome in the next 20 years. It is a commonplace that, following the closure of many long-term psychiatric hospitals, prisons have become the place of refuge and asylum for those unable to 'benefit' from care in the community. At least two prisons (Downview in Sutton, Surrey, and Parc in Bridgend, South Wales) are actually built on the sites of former psychiatric hospitals, and it seems certain that some of their former residents will have returned under a different guise. Care in the community has all too often meant an absence of care and the uncertain use of prescribed anti-psychotic medication. Prisons have once more become frontline mental health facilities.

If we are optimistic, we might conclude that it will become increasingly possible to transfer those with the most severe psychotic illnesses into mainstream psychiatric provision (the number of such transfers is already at record levels, albeit lagging behind the need). However, it is fanciful to believe that those prisoners with less severe symptoms, or with low-level depressive illnesses, will not remain the responsibility of the Prison Service. Although I have judged that prison healthcare has come on by leaps and bounds in recent years, the pressures of delivering high quality primary care with such a physically and mentally vulnerable population will continue to increase. One prisoner in every eleven asks to see the doctor every day. This is not like primary care in the average GP's surgery.

I note that the psychiatric profession is itself changing and practitioners are increasingly convinced of the organic roots of psychiatric disturbance. Given that treatment may not be given compulsorily in prison, it may be that this will encourage greater investment in medium secure psychiatric facilities or in other hybrid institutions combining aspects of custody and mental health care. (And to speculate more wildly—and perhaps more damagingly to my reputation— I wonder if people will start to become as interested in the organic roots, if there are such, of criminal behaviour. For example, I have always been intrigued by the putative link between diet and offending behaviour. The Victorians had a pseudo-science called phrenology that attempted to identify and categorise offenders on the basis of the shape of their skulls. Modern-day phrenology would look at the brain chemistry within those skulls and the twists and turns of DNA.)

Many of those deemed to be suffering from a personality disorder rather than a mainstream mental illness will also continue to be the responsibility of the prisons. My expectation is that we will see an expansion of units like the Dangerous and Severe Personality Disorder units at Whitemoor, Frankland, Broadmoor and Rampton which, as I noted earlier, have proved to be a British success story. Indeed, it may be that those whose personality disorders are somewhat less dangerous (readers may recall from what I wrote earlier that there is a bewildering array of diagnosed personality disorders) will also benefit from the development of specialist units. The use of specialist units is an area where the Prison Service has a good deal of experience, and a pretty good tale to tell.

More generally, you could make a reasonable case for saying the Prison Service has become the backstop for every other public service. It provides healthcare for those who never register with a doctor or dentist. It provides education for those who have dropped out, or been excluded, from school. It provides kindness and support for those who have never known a loving family. It offers job training to those who have never had paid employment. It offers drug and alcohol detoxification for those whose lives are wrecked by an addiction. (It detoxifies thousands, probably tens of thousands of people each year. Compare that with drug agencies in the community.) The history of the prison system is a mirror image of the history of the welfare state. As welfarism becomes politically and economically less attractive, it is the Prison Service that picks up the pieces. It is the welfare state's default option.

CHAPTER 8

Final Thoughts

CHAPTER 8

Final Thoughts

Although largely unacknowledged—save on the part of former Home Secretary Michael Howard—a political belief in the power of prison in delivering incapacitation to ensure public protection has been one of the drivers of penal policy since the mid-1990s. In other words, despite its costs and the acknowledged damage that it does to individual prisoners and their families, simply keeping people off the streets is seen as a pretty good bargain. (The argument would be that, whatever their reconviction rate after release, for the period of their imprisonment prisoners have a reconviction rate approaching zero. Although it may sound rather Zen to say so, these are 'real' non-crimes. In other words, they reduce the total volume of crime, notwithstanding that on release prisoners may well be more handicapped in leading crime-free lives than if they had been punished in the community.) The case for incapacitation has been very persuasive in the United States until the point where the costs to the local taxpayer have become absolutely excessive. In practice, it has proved increasingly persuasive in this country too. Whether acknowledged or not, I believe that it will continue to hold sway.

Let us pursue the argument a little further. Let us take what is achieved through incapacitation, add some rehabilitative effect as well (for all but very short-term prisoners), and then take into account that lots of community penalties are actually quite expensive. If someone is subject to intensive probation-style supervision with a bit of tagging on top, this does not come cheap—either in terms of marginal or average costs. In contrast, the marginal costs of prison sentences are quite low—at least until such point as new prisons and new staff are required. Those of us who regard prisons as an unfortunate social necessity, and who have an intuitive dislike for States where there is too much imprisonment, have found ourselves on the wrong side of history here too.

Nevertheless, the moral performance of prisons—the decency agenda, the attempts to measure the quality of prison life—will thankfully remain a concern for anyone who sees imprisonment as being about more than security and the achievement of key performance indicators. It will remain a people business—and we will continue to employ a lot of staff by comparison to American prisons in particular. This seems to accord with public sentiment too. However, the temptation to replace staff with technology will I think be one of the themes of the next 20 years.

How will our prisons be organized? The idea of foundation prisons—by analogy to the foundation hospitals which are part of the NHS but are essentially self-governing—represents an aspect of current Conservative Party thinking. I think this will have some mileage. Indeed, it is a perfectly proper objective to try to make prisons more self-governing, and more responsive to their local community, within an overall national framework of rules and standards. The question of whether prisons should remain a nationally run service, or whether they can become more local or more regional, is likely to be one of the emerging themes over the next two decades. Can gaols opt out of the Prison Service monolith (and if so, which gaols?) Can they become more locally responsible (thus, taking us back to the days before nationalisation in the 1870s)? What would be the effect if Governors were much more in charge of their own performance?

I am certain that we will continue with a mixed economy. Both main political parties believe in such an approach, with private prisons leading the way and public prisons reorganizing their methods and their workforce to deliver cost-savings and 'value for money'. Likewise, both political parties are committed to splitting between the purchaser and provider functions in criminal justice services, just as has been done in the NHS. The model to which the NOMS agency is currently working (NOMS 2) is clearly predicated upon the commissioning of services, and commissioning becomes meaningless unless there is competition. The private companies have now entered the mainstream, and their prospects are more rosy than at any time for over a decade. (The techniques they have used to enter the mainstream are worthy of research. If you attend the annual Koestler Awards exhibition for prisoners' art, it is striking how many of the prizes are sponsored by the private companies.) I see no reason to believe other than that the private sector is going to grow as a proportion of the prison system as a whole. Privatisation is here to stay (something that no one would have predicted in 1980 when it was another word that had hardly been invented).

A mixed economy also embraces the idea that prisons, probation, parole and tagging will all come closer together. The directors of offender management (DOMS) are going to be key players in all of this. I have some doubts about the latest structure in terms of how much support it will offer to prison Governors, the governance of probation, and whether the NOMS brand will have to go. But there is no question that the NOMS 2 model has got more life in it than there ever was in NOMS 1, a purchaser-provider split but a textbook example of how a major programme of change can be thrown into disarray by the rapid turnover of politicians and officials. NOMS 1 was predicated on capping the prison population at 80,000 and driving up effectiveness through competition. Whatever their merits, these were policies agreed by David Blunkett but abandoned by his successor, Charles Clarke, within weeks of his appointment as Home Secretary.

So does all of this represent, as I suggested at the beginning of this short book, something approaching an end to prison history? Remember please that the end of history is not intended to imply the end of events; there will always be new crises, new challenges, and new initiatives. But have we now reached a broadly steady state? It is manifest that prisons are physically better places than what they were in 1980. The daily practice of slopping-out is no more. There are no mental healthcare facilities in prison which are remotely as disgusting as they used to be. The daily treatment of prisoners is fairer, more just, more equitable. There is much more engagement with the idea of helping people lead more socially acceptable, more personally rewarding, more crime-free lives on release.

It is also manifest that there is a political consensus that punishment has its place, and that prison is the legitimate and leading vehicle through which punishment is delivered. This shared political commitment to the prison as a socially desirable institution has helped drive the increase in the prison population over the last 20 years. And, as I have noted, when there are few ideological differences between political parties competing in a democracy, the politicisation of crime is probably inevitable. Certainly, and with very few exceptions, it is an international phenomenon and perhaps irreversible. After all, you can never have too little crime, and crime rates can never be low enough. Indeed, if you look hard enough you can always find some more crime—whether in the home, the school or the workplace. Most minor incivility does not currently find its way into the crime statistics (not that there would be any merit were it to do so).

Temperamentally I am an optimist. I hope therefore that prisons can cease to be driven by a simplistic political-media agenda. I hope that the costs and pains of the excessive use of imprisonment will come to be seen as disproportionate, divisive, and ultimately self-defeating. I hope that the problems of crime and crime prevention will be given their social and moral dimensions. I hope that resources currently devoted to imprisonment can be re-directed towards investment in the community. I hope that restorative approaches to criminal behaviour can become the norm not the exception. And I hope that tolerance and understanding will regain their status as exemplars of a good and mature society. (In a rare contribution to penological debate, the former Prime Minister, John Major, opined that we should 'condemn a little more and understand a little less'. I followed ten years after Mr Major into Rutlish School, Merton, in South London. The better of my teachers taught me to take the entirely opposite view.)

However, what we hope for and what we receive are two entirely different things, and they have little place in a history. It seems to me that what Fukuyama called the triumph of liberal democracy has indeed resulted in less tolerance of those at the margins of society, and a growing faith in the value of incarceration. Despite the financial drain that imprisonment represents to the Exchequer, the prison population seems set to rise still further as we head towards 2030.

But less tolerance of crime does not mean a return to the penal decrepitude and unpleasantness all too common in 1980. So far as the Prison Service is concerned, I think that the future consists of broadly decent prisons, provided by a mix of public and private suppliers. There will be more use of technology, more focus on the effectiveness of regimes and interventions, more competition between gaols. The prisons will probably be large, and prisoners' lives more regulated both in custody and on release. And the prison population will continue its six-decade upward trend, fed as ever by the poor, the mentally ill, and the marginalised minorities. It is the end of prison history. Unless we make it otherwise.

Some works, reports and sources mentioned in the text

Borstal Boy (1958), Brendan Behan, Hutchinson

Criminal Justice Act 1948

Criminal Justice Act 1991

English Prisons Today: Being the Report of the Prison System Enquiry Committee (1922), Edited by Stephen Hobhouse and Fenner Brockway, Green & Co

'Factors Linked to Re-offending: A One-year Follow-up of Prisoners Who Took Part in the Resettlement Surveys 2001, 2003 and 2004' (2008), Ministry of Justice

Gladstone Report (1895)

Learmont Report (1995)

Prison Act 1877

Probation of Offenders Act 1907

Soledad Brother: The Prison Letters of George Jackson (1970), George Jackson, Jean Genet and Jonathan Jackson, Lawrence Hill Books

Woodcock Report (1994)

Woolf Report (1991)

The Downing Street Years (1995 (new edn.)), Margaret Thatcher, HarperCollins

The End of History and the Last Man (1992), Francis Fukuyama, Penguin

The Loneliness of the Long Distance Runner (1959), Alan Sillitoe, HarperPerennial (re-issue edn. 2007)

The State of the Prisons in England and Wales (1777), John Howard

Index

anti-racism *59*
 hidden racist under-
  current *59*
 race equality *59*
 tolerance and inte-
  gration *98*
radicalisation *97*
Radzinowicz, Leon *25*
Rampton *100*
'Rat-Boy' *28*
rate of imprisonment *78*
razor wire *85*
recall to prison *95*
reconviction rates *47, 62, 105*
reduction in privilege
  level *83*
reform *20, 64, 79*
 reforming Gover-
  nors, etc. *55*
 social reformers of
  100 years ago *49*
 women's prisons *79*
'refractory' behaviour *26*
refuge *98*
regimes *57, 62, 63, 87, 91, 110*
 regime hours *86*
 treatment regime *84*
 under growing threat *86*
regulation *69, 83, 110*
rehabilitation *viii, 20,*
  28, 87, 105

sympathy for rehabilita-
  tive approach *65*
release *76, 84, 95, 105, 108*
 early release *84*
 post-release super-
  vision *62*
religious aspects *37,*
  77, 96, 97
remand *37*
re-offending *viii, 61*
resettlement *61, 70*
resources *43, 60, 70, 73,*
  87, 91, 109
 financial squeeze *86*
respect *71*
restorative approaches *109*
restrictions on life, liberty
  and property *34*
rhetoric *51, 59, 80*
risk *73, 74, 84, 87*
Ruggles-Brise, Evelyn *27*
rules, standards, orders and
  instructions *56*
Russians *77*
safety *87, 91*
 keeping prisoners
  safely occupied *91*
 'safer custody' *75*
sanitation *57*
Sartre, Jean Paul *35*
saving taxpayers' money *73*